Paper Dandy's

HORRORGAMI
20 Gruesome Scenes to Cut and Fold

Marc Hagan-Guirey

Laurence King Publishing

In memory of Mum

———

LAURENCE KING

Published in 2015 by
Laurence King Publishing Ltd
361–373 City Road
London EC1V 1LR
e-mail: enquiries@laurenceking.com
www.laurenceking.com

Reprinted 2016

© Marc Hagan-Guirey
This book was designed and produced by
Laurence King Publishing Ltd, London.

Marc Hagan-Guirey has asserted his right under
the Copyright, Designs and Patents Act of 1988 to
be identified as the author of this work.

A catalogue record for this book is available
from the British Library.

ISBN: 978-1-78067-593-0

Design: Charlotte Klingholz
Senior Editor: Peter Jones

Printed in China

———

Thank you
My lovely family: Barry, Lorinda, Cathy, Eamon, John and
the kids Molly, Jacob, Harry and the new one.

My school art teacher Fiona McAveery and my university
course tutor Susan Platt – Catherine Collins and Gallery
One and a Half for making the Horrorgami exhibition
a reality.

Lex.

Everyone at Laurence King for giving me the opportunity
to make this book – especially Lewis, Sarah and Peter

And Derren, thank you.

Contents

Introduction

Decorex Palace: photographed by John Godwin
www.john-godwin.co.uk

Horrorgami is a combination of several different passions of mine: horror, craft and architecture.

Long before I started making horrorgami or had even seen my first horror film my greatest joy was (and still is) making stuff. I wasn't a sporty or terribly confident child. At times I was very solitary but I was happiest when I was just being. I'd happily while away my days 'making and doing' and my currency was egg cartons, toilet roll tubes and cereal boxes. The weekly shopping would hardly have been in the cupboards five minutes before I'd have bartered for cereal boxes in exchange for household tasks. My mum eventually accepted this and invested in a lot of Tupperware. Times were often really tough financially for us when I was growing up but somehow my mum made ends meet and

always managed to provide me with the latest 'must-have' action figures – He-Man, ThunderCats and Defenders of the Earth – you name it, I had it. On Christmases and birthdays I'd come down to the sitting room to find Skeletor and his henchmen already free from their blister packs and set up in a ready-made battle scene. I knew we weren't well-off but I never really questioned how she managed to afford all of these toys until I asked her years later. I grew up in Northern Ireland in the '80s during the 'Troubles'. Explosions often gutted entire department stores and my mum, being the thrifty genius she was, would go to these shops and rummage through the fire-damaged goods. She'd buy the whole set of figures, discard the charred packaging and wash them until they looked like new. I knew no different. 'Nice one,' I'd think, 'no need to waste time on opening them – commence epic battle for the secrets of Grayskull'! But therein lay the problem. I didn't have Castle Grayskull, so I'd turn to my stash of cardboard goods and set about crafting a fortress to my own design. I'm certain that's where my love of architecture stems from.

My elder brother and I were very different characters growing up. He was boisterous and sporty, I was timid and creative; but the one thing that really bonded us was our love of horror. A by-product of growing up in a staunchly Catholic town was that superstition was heavily engrained into society. It was a very simple equation: If God exists, then there must be such a thing as the Devil. This, of course, was proof that there are such things as demons, ghosts, spirits and possessions – standard childhood interests. I found this a much more interesting aspect of religion and I'm certain this is the only reason I identified myself as 'spiritual' until my 20s. Our town was rife with urban legend and reported hauntings. I could write another book on the tales of the 'White Hoods', a rumoured satanic cult that terrorized my hometown, or the 'Hatchet Man', a garden-tool-wielding maniac who would roam the streets seeking revenge on the anniversary of his death. We loved it and from that grew an appetite that was relatively satiated by horror films. Whether or not my brother garnered a secret satisfaction from seeing the wits scared out of me is still up for discussion, but either way, while on babysitting duty he'd allow me to stay up late and watch films far beyond my age – *Amityville*, *The Exorcist*, *Psycho*. I think I'd seen most of them before I was a teenager. I've since come to terms with the fact that there are no such things as spirits, be they holy or horror, but my love of the idea of them shows no sign of dying.

Over the years my knowledge of architecture became slightly broader than cartoon characters' hideouts. In particular, I've always found Art Deco and Mid-Century buildings captivating and I focused on the work of Frank Lloyd Wright. When I visited Los Angeles in 2010, my friend and partner had arranged for me to be shown around my favourite of Frank Lloyd Wright's buildings: the Ennis House, designed in 1923. Movie buffs will recognize it as the exterior to Deckard's apartment in *Blade Runner*. It's also the exterior to the mansion in *House on Haunted Hill,* a 1959 horror film starring Vincent Price. The building had long been in a state of disrepair and in 1994 a hugely damaging earthquake left it barely clinging to the hill upon which it had been built. Later, a charity that tried to restore it ran out of money and was forced to put it

on the market for $15 million. The building had been out of bounds to the public for some 20 years and, scheming duo that we were, we seized this as an opportunity to get me through the door. I was blissfully unaware until we pulled up outside its gates. So as we calmly walked around, asking the usual enquiries about the plumbing and the state of the electrics, my heart was in my mouth – I was half terrified of being found out and half completely overwhelmed by what was happening. On reflection, it's the closest thing I ever had to a 'real' spiritual experience. On returning home I wanted to make something to commemorate the experience and I set my mind to creating a model of the house. That's when I came across the art of kirigami. The fragility of the building and the delicacy of paper felt like a good fit for a replica. The reaction to the model was really positive and I'd already decided what to move on to next.

I'm completely obsessed with all things Addams Family and because of my love of architecture and the macabre this manifested as a life-long fixation with their decaying Second Empire mansion – especially the one from the 1991 film version. The house, almost a character in its own right, is an omnipresent, sprawling mass of innumerable rooms, sweeping split staircases, secret doors and cavernous underground vaults, its Art Nouveau detailing long past the point of restoration. Not exactly your usual 'dream home' material, but it was mine. Growing up, I'd attempted to make models with whatever I could lay my hands on. I still have an ongoing project of trying to create an accurate set of floorplans of the Addams house. I've even gone to the extent of 'freeze-framing' every interior clip in the film to try and piece together the layout. Through a bit of online snooping, I managed to acquire the email address of the art director who designed the house, Larry Hubbs. I nervously wrote him an email (he was a childhood hero, after all) with some photos attached of the kirigami. To my surprise, a few weeks later I received a response: he loved it and in his reply he sent me scans of his original elevation drawings. He also apologized that he no longer had the floorplans but made some amendments to the scheme I'd worked out during my freeze-framing efforts. I was beside myself with excitement. Needless to say, I sent him a model, which he tells me sits on his desk at home.

On completion of the Addams house it struck me that I'd made two 'haunted' movie houses. I realized that my love of horror and architecture had a new creative outlet and Horrorgami was born. Coincidentally I'd just resigned from my three-and-a-half-year post as head of studio at an advertising agency and the project I was due to move on to was suddenly cancelled, meaning that I was jobless. While I was deciding what my next move was, I kept working on Horrorgami. It was around this time that I was introduced to Catherine Collins, the owner of Gallery One and a Half in Hackney, East London. 'Horrorgami' – a collection of 13 kirigami models based on haunted locations from film and TV opened to the public on Hallowe'en night 2012.

News of 'Horrorgami' went viral and a result of that has been that I've been lucky enough to continue making pieces for clients such as Samsung, P&G and Decorex International. One of my proudest moments was creating

a piece for the Terrence Higgins Trust to be sold as part of a charity auction at Christie's in March 2014. The piece, called Soho Uncut, sold for £19,000 and every penny was donated to the charity. I couldn't believe that something like this had grown from a hobby.

Traditionally kirigami has been used to make models of buildings like the Empire State Building or the Eiffel Tower. As beautiful as they are, I felt there was an opportunity to do something more. For me the art form is more than just paper craft. It's about theatre, storytelling and creating an engaging visual for a viewer to get lost in. I get so much joy from sitting in my studio, meticulously crafting tiny worlds for you to peer into. And when I think about it, nothing much has changed – I'm still that quiet kid who'd unravel the remaining toilet paper for the cardboard tube and decant cornflakes into plastic containers for the box, all so that I could sit content making paper fortresses. The only difference now is that I get to share them with you.

How to Use This Book

Preparation is essential in successful horrorgami. Ensure that you have everything you need within reach and make sure you're working in a well-lit room. Try to wear short sleeves and lose any bracelets that might snag on paper elements. Take your time and have lots of breaks. Cutting on such a small scale can be quite intense. If you accidentally cut something incorrectly, don't despair. Finish the model and use a bit of sticky tape to put it back together. If you preserve the templates, you can try again when ready.

Tools and materials

Bone folder – Not essential but creates nice crisp folds.

Scalpel and blades – Buy blades in bulk and always use a sharp one.

Metal ruler – Plastic rulers get damaged by sharp knives and rarely have a true straight edge. Keep the ruler clean.

Paper – Templates in this book are printed on 200 g/m². If you want to keep the book intact, scan or photocopy the model and reprint it on a paper stock of 180–220 g/m².

Self-healing cutting mat – Protects the work surface and prolongs the life of your blades.

Skewers or toothpicks – Use for popping out small creases or to keep a fold from inverting in on itself as you fold opposing planes.

Terminology

Familiarize yourself with these terms for the folding instructions.

The background plane – The 'sky' and vertical standing section of the model.

The base plane – The floor or ground on which the model stands.

Façades – The vertical 'walls' of the model, usually forward-facing, they might feature doors or windows.

The horizon – The main, 90-degree fold that forms the flat base which the model sits on

and the vertical upright part of the model. The most outer fold, the horizon is usually the starting point for folding.

Roof planes – The model's horizontal roofs.

Structural lines – Printed here in black, these are the lines that you cut through completely.

The template is printed on the reverse of the model, so the printed side of the template will be the reverse of the design in the photos. The display side of the model is the blank side of the paper.

Cutting, scoring and folding

I find it best to work from the centre of the model and move outwards. Next I move on to details such as a character's outlines – anything that isn't a straight line.

Then I cut the structural lines. There is often a lot of detailing on structural lines. Only use these as a guide. As long as you're cutting in the general direction of the line, the model will still work.

Half-cutting

Half-cutting means scoring a line that only cuts halfway through the paper, making it fold and creating a hinge at 90 degrees. Reserve a blunt blade for half-cutting.

Mountain and valley folds

Half-cut valley folds (green dotted and dashed lines) on the reverse (printed) side of the template. The fold is pushed inwards like a valley. Mountain folds (orange lines), the opposite, are half-scored on the front, the non-printed (display) side and then

pushed outwards. The horizon fold of the model is always a valley fold. Folds are referred to as they are viewed from the front (display side) of the model. When folding a valley fold from behind we'll still refer to it as the valley fold.

Marking mountain scores

Only one side of the paper is printed, which is fine for seeing where you need to cut and perform half-score valley folds, therefore you'll need to make some small incisions on the back of the card marking out where you need to perform half-score for mountain folds on the front. On the printed side of the template, use the tip of the blade to make a small incision on both ends of the orange dotted mountain fold line. When you flip the paper over, you'll see the two small holes. Line up your ruler between these points and half-score. For longer mountain folds create one or two markers along the length of the line.

Progressive folding

Never crease the folds sharply in the first instance. Apply a little pressure and help them move in the direction you want. Gently work your way around the various folds of the model; return to the beginning and apply more pressure to the crease each time. Do this two or three times before the model is complete. This is progressive folding. The breaking point of the paper is where the crease becomes 'memory'. Successful folding of horrorgami relies on the various valley and mountain folds being correctly half-cut before you begin folding. Double-check that you've completed all the half-scoring before you start folding.

Folding techniques

Often the best method for folding a crease will feel very intuitive. Shown here are a few techniques used in the folding instructions. The later models will assume you've picked up techniques and terminology from the beginner models so it is a good idea to work your way through the book.

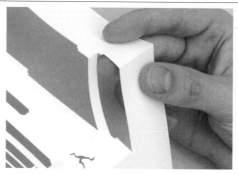

Levering – Using your middle finger behind the fold as a lever, push down the background plane with your forefinger and the base plane with your thumb.

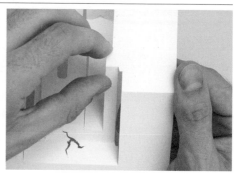

Pinching – Although I rarely recommend pinching the crease, it is sometimes useful on smaller mountain or valley folds.

Pushing out – Holding the model in one hand, use the fingers of the other to push one side of the paper along the fold. You'll have to gradually work along the fold in some cases. Mainly used for valley folds.

Skewer – Use a skewer and the same technique as levering to pop elements out in a space too small to fit your finger in.

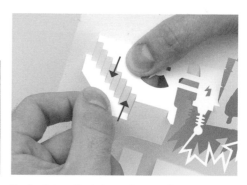

Springing – Push two planes of paper on the same axis together by holding a plane in each hand and moving them in opposite directions. Allow the paper to spring back to its original position, repeat several times, working the folds until they go past their breaking point and become memory. This is very useful for folding stairs.

The Thing under the Stairs

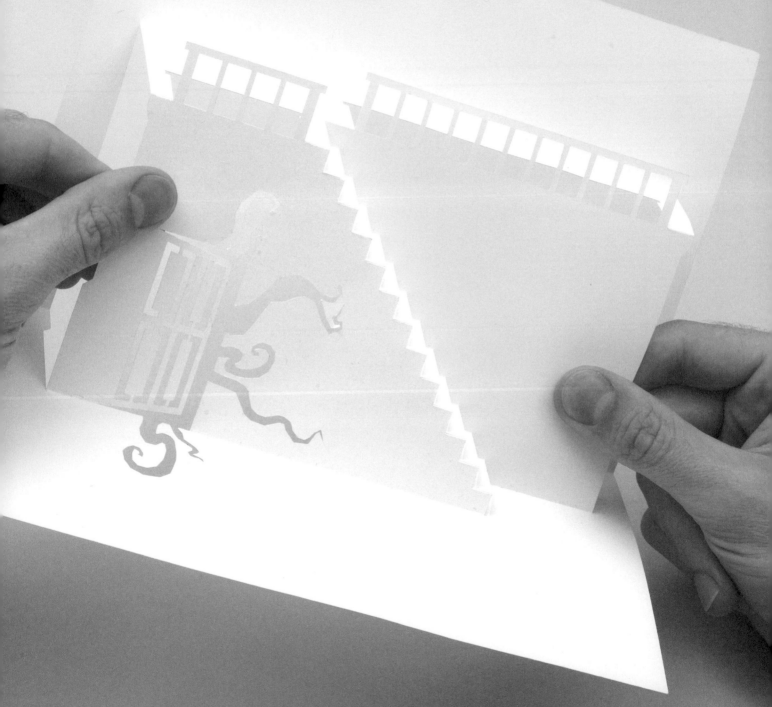

01 The Thing under the Stairs

Difficulty level: Beginner

There's something under the stairs and whatever it is, it's not from this world. This horrorgami depicts the dreadful being I used to invent as a kid that lingered in the darkness. Being the strange child that I was, I wanted to investigate rather than flee, but this all changed on Hallowe'en 1992. Home alone, I turned on the television. If you're a child of the '80s, you might remember *Ghost Watch*, a BBC 'mockumentary' that aired on 31 October that year. It was presented as a live TV broadcast from a reportedly haunted suburban house in the UK. The house was monitored using 'ghost-detecting equipment' and the family occupants were interviewed about their experiences. At the beginning of the show there was a hint that it was a piece of fiction, but the vast majority of viewers were convinced that it was a real event unfolding before their eyes. The malevolent force within the house, which gradually made more appearances as the show progressed, was nicknamed Pipes; it had trapped a girl in a cupboard under the stairs.

This was the most traumatic piece of television I'd ever seen. I was found by my neighbour sobbing on the doorstep of our house, too afraid to be inside by myself. If you haven't seen it, hunt down a copy because essentially this show is the original *Paranormal Activity* (2007) and spawned an entire genre of 'found footage' films.

The model is simple architecturally but is really effective. Staircases tend to be the most impressive part of kirigami models; here, the angle at which the door is set and the way that the tentacles creep through it help give a narrative to an otherwise static structure.

Cutting tips

Start with the door and the tentacles. Take your time with the tentacles. You can always freestyle them if you're not that confident. The railings will take a little time but once you're done, the final product will quickly take shape.

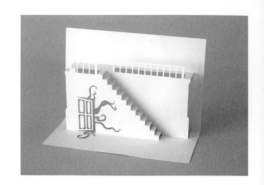

Folding

With the printed side facing up, start by folding the horizons. Place your index finger in the valley of the fold while pushing your thumb and forefinger down. This is called levering.

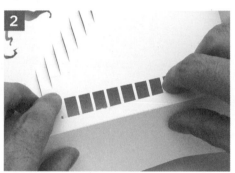

Rotate the paper 180 degrees. Push out the long valley fold that joins the top of the landing to the background. This time you can use a clawing technique to close the fold. Clawing is like pinching but you can use more than just finger and thumb.

Push out the valley fold that joins up the front façade of the stairs and the wall behind it. Use your index finger as a lever by placing it in the valley of the fold while pushing the front façade and base down over it using the forefinger and thumb of your other hand.

Flip the paper over and crease the mountain folds of the landing and landing area at the top of the stairs. Again, levering works best here (A).

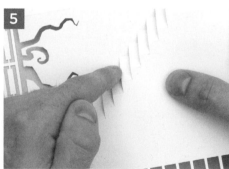

Work on folding the mountain and valley folds of the staircase with the push-out technique – hold the section illustrated in one hand and push out the backs of the steps to create a 90-degree angle between the top and back planes of the paper. Flip the paper over and do the other side.

Use the springing technique to fold all of the staircase elements evenly and at the same time. In this case hold the two façades between your forefingers and thumbs and push them in opposite directions but together. Use a springing action, applying a little more pressure each time. Close the entire model flat along it's horizon. Unfold to display your first horrorgami model.

Crypt Creeping

02 Crypt Creeping
Difficulty level: Beginner

On the street where I grew up there were two graveyards to choose from, both of which were considered forbidden territory. One in particular looked as if it had been the inspiration for every Hammer Horror movie graveyard scene, as it was eternally bathed in an oppressive mist. It lay at the bottom of a very long, steep lane. The farther down the lane towards the gates you went, the taller the bowing dry-stone walls that flanked the length of it appeared. For my friends and me, visiting graveyards on Secret Seven-style missions was as much (if not more) about hunting for demonic spirits as about showing respect for the dead.

Almost every headstone in this graveyard was crooked and decayed. They sank in soft, marshy ground and tombs with huge gaping cracks right across the middle collapsed inwards. We'd take note of surnames and somehow create a tenuous link back to urban legends. Having quite active imaginations, we made connections with the satanic cult of the White Hoods that tormented our hometown, or with the Hatchet Man (see page 6). As we worked ourselves up into a complete frenzy, half excited, half fearful, any unexpected sound would send us scrambling in sheer panic back to the gates. And just like in a nightmare, the lane would appear to grow longer and steeper the farther and faster you ran. Utter terror. Oh, to be young again!

Cutting tips

This horrorgami is quite straightforward; lots of nice straight edges. Obviously the picket gate will take some time and patience. Use a ruler for the most part but you should be OK cutting freehand around the pickets. Although I'd normally suggest cutting the details such as the cracks first, on this occasion I'd start by cutting the gate, then the rest of the model, and finally the cracking detail. Feel free to add more cracks.

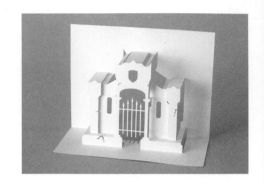

Folding

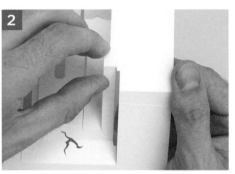

1 With the printed side facing you, start by folding the main horizon crease, using the levering technique. Push down the background plane with your forefinger and the base plane with your thumb while placing your middle finger in the valley of the fold for leverage.

2 Just above both of the horizon folds are more valley folds connecting the base to the back plane. Apply a light pinching to them while holding the horizon as you were before (levering technique). They naturally want to move into shape, so you just need a small amount of pressure to help them on their way (A).

3 Crease the valley folds that form the base of the tomb. Put the forefinger of one hand behind the card in the valley of the fold and use the forefinger and thumb of your other hand to push. Next, fold the valley folds immediately above using the same method (B).

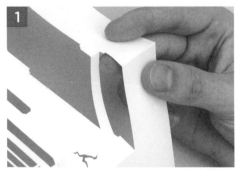

4 Still with the printed side of the paper facing you, rotate the page 180 degrees and work across the seven valley folds that connect the roof of the tomb to the background using the push-out technique – hold the horrorgami in one hand and place the fingers of the same hand into the crease of the fold you're working on. Use your other hand to push out the folds.

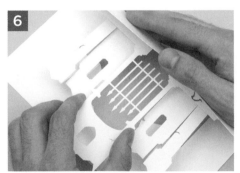

5 Turn the paper over and, starting from the bottom working upwards, fold all of the mountain folds – the base (push out), the two pillars on the left and right (lever fold) and the roof connections (push out). Leave the very small areas that connect the two front columns to the body of the tomb until the end. They'll naturally take shape but only after you've been around everything for a second time.

6 Fold the model flat before opening it up to display. It's a good idea to guide the front gate section by pulling it gently with one hand as you're doing this because the columns are quite narrow and may buckle.

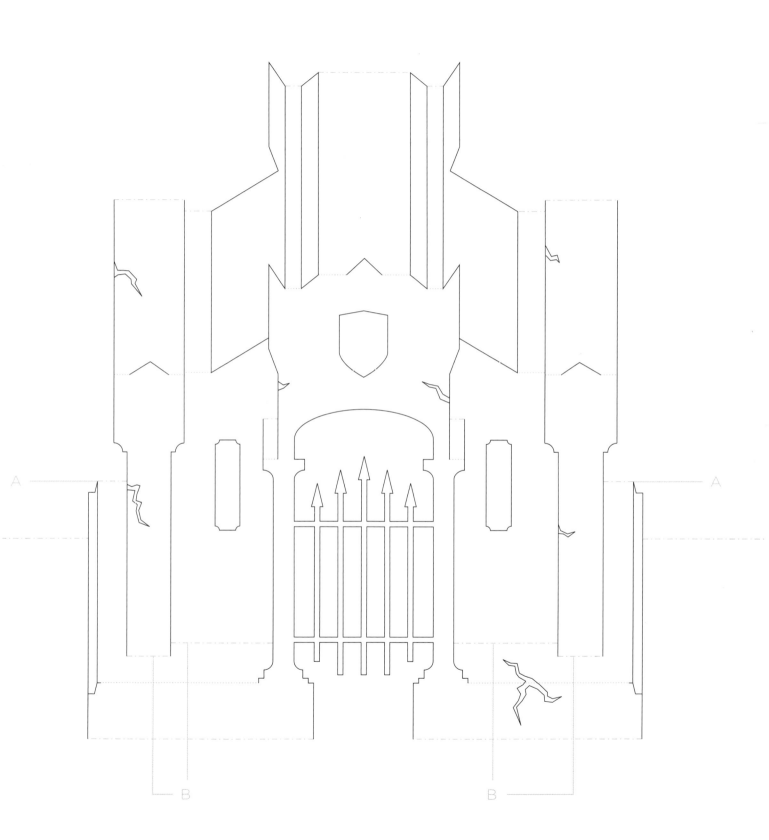

Suburban Slaughter

03 Suburban Slaughter

Difficulty level: Beginner

This horrorgami is based on the house from Wes Craven's *A Nightmare on Elm Street* in which Nancy Thompson and her schoolfriends' dreams are invaded by one of the most infamous characters in horror – Freddy Krueger, the bladed glove-wearing child murderer. Released in 1984, *A Nightmare on Elm Street* is a must-see for all budding horror aficionados even if it's just to see a young Johnny Depp in his first big screen role essentially got blended in his bedroom. It works for me.

The fictional number 1428 Elm Street, Springwood, was shot on location at 1428 N Genesee Ave, Los Angeles. The real house was used in the first two films of the series (constructed sets were used for the later films) and it is still standing. By searching online you can see how a recent owner completely remodelled it, turning it from a house of hell into a much less gruesome affair. As a nod to the house's role in the film, the new owners painted the door red, as it was in the series.

Cutting tips

Start by cutting out the character in the doorway. Don't feel that you have to cut around him in one movement of the blade. It's easier if you approach it as a lot of small, straight lines in a sequence. Make a small incision, then lift the blade, then place the blade back on the paper again for the next cut, and so on. After you've cut him out, it shouldn't be too much of a 'nightmare' to finish.

Folding

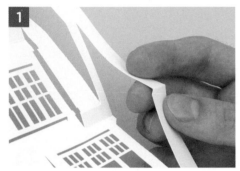

With the printed side facing you, start by folding the main horizon crease, using the levering technique. Push down the background plane with your forefinger and the base plane with your thumb while placing your middle finger in the valley of the fold for leverage.

Push out the valley folds on the base of the house, followed by the porch step.

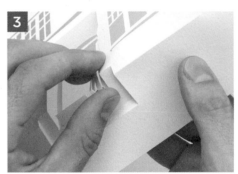

Work on the valley folds where the porch is joined to the front of the house. Only do this a little the first time and come back to it at a later stage to apply more pressure to the crease. Next, push out the pillars of the porch and the character's feet.

Rotate the model 180 degrees and push out the valley fold that joins the roof to the background plane, then move on to the valley folds around the roof area and to the top of the porch.

With the model on its side, work down the folds at the top of the dormer window. Refer to the image above – essentially you're using your fingers to push the creases into each other.

Use a skewer against the back of the mountain fold for the step of the front porch. You can then push the step flat against the base to complete the crease.

The Fall of the House of Usher

04 The Fall of the House of Usher

Difficulty level: Beginner

When I was younger, I had a copy of *Tales of Mystery and Terror*, a collection of Edgar Allan Poe's short stories. My obsession with architecture must have already been well established as I remember becoming quite fixated with 'The Fall of the House of Usher', with the house playing as important a role as the characters in the story. The narrator describes the house as giving him a 'sense of insufferable gloom'. Beyond mention of a dense fungi covering the walls and, of course, a fine zigzagged fissure running from the roof to the ground that would go unrecognized to most, the physical description of the house is sparing. As a youngster, I imagined what the façade of the building would look like: a lonely and imposing house that even the architect found despair in creating. There's also mention of eye-like windows. I imagined them sitting above the main doorway within a central tower, like a cluster of tiny arachnid eyes, poised and waiting. It's about time I turned this memory into a horrorgami for you to tear apart at your own will.

Cutting tips

The beauty of this horrorgami is its simplicity that gives the cracking effect centre stage. I've kept the lines as simple and as straight as possible so you can put your energy into cutting the crack. Be careful not to cut the whole way through the central window set.

Folding

1 Start with the printed side facing you and lever-fold the two main valley folds.

2 Next, turn your attention to the three valley folds that form the base of the building. Hold the base plane of the model in one hand and, with as many fingers as possible of the other hand, push out the façade of the building to create the crease, working from one side to the other.

3 Rotate the model 180 degrees and apply the same technique here to crease the valley folds that join the roof to the background plane.

4 With the model in the same orientation, lever-fold the two valley folds (one on the left and one on the right) that join the lower roof to the background plane.

5 Now flip the template over and fold the mountain folds at the top of the roof. Again, using a lever fold is best here for the ends. You can apply a soft pinch to help fold the central part of the roof.

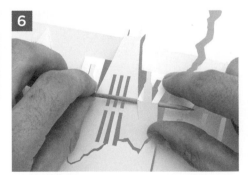

6 The final section involves folding the various mountain and valley folds where the top of the building's façade and the base of the roof meet (A). Using a skewer will help 'pop' out the mountain folds. You'll have to apply a folding technique that feels right. Don't expect to complete the crease past breaking point the first time. Work your way around the model a few times before folding it flat.

A

Gallows Hill

05 Gallows Hill

Difficulty level: Beginner

Perched on top of a very steep climb is another one of the places where I used to play as a child – Heather Park in Newry, Northern Ireland. Despite the uninterrupted views of the town below, the site has a darker history, for this hilltop was also the site of the old town gallows, giving the park the more sinister name by which it's still more commonly known – Gallows Hill.

The tunnel through which the accused would be led, from the 'gaol' at the bottom of the hill, is still partially intact – unnervingly sitting only yards from a set of swings. Down a series of sunken steps an iron gate blocks the entrance to the pitch-black tunnel. As children, groups of us were able to squeeze our scrawny frames through the top of the bars and down the dank passageway into the darkness. Petrified doesn't cover the emotions I'd experience as we crept single-file to the section which opened up to ground level. I have a distinct memory of the relief I would experience on seeing daylight when emerging from the dark. It always struck me that this feeling would have been the complete antithesis to that felt by the poor souls being lead in the opposite direction to their execution.

Cutting tips

The trickiest part of this horrorgami is the very thin hanging rope. Cut that area last even after doing the scoring on both sides. You just want to minimize the amount of time it's loose and prone to accidentally creasing or breaking. Cut it as thinly as you feel comfortable with and keep your eye on this section at all times during the folding stage.

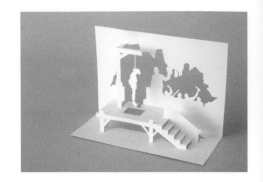

Folding

Hold the base plane in one hand with the printed side of the card facing you. With a finger of the other hand, push out the valley folds at the base of the platform. Apply a little pressure to the base of the staircase and the handrail behind it – but not too much at this stage.

Using the lever-fold technique, crease the two main horizon valley folds.

Rotate the model 180 degrees and hold it at the top. Use a finger of your other hand to push out the valley fold of the connecting plane that joins the top of the gallows to the background plane. You'll only need to apply a little pressure here, as the paper will begin to fold under the weight.

Make the valley folds of the platform surface, holding the paper with your thumb through the hole that was created from cutting out the jeering crowd.

Turn the paper over and make the mountain fold at the top of the gallows. Be really careful here so that you don't snag the rope on anything. It's OK to pinch this crease all the way.

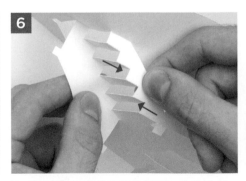

Use the springing technique to fold the stairs. Hold the railings between thumb and forefinger of one hand; hold the façade of the staircase with the other hand. Put your index finger under the stairs and gently push the elements together in a springing motion, a little each time until the creases become more permanent. Crease the mountain fold along the top of the platform, then stand the model upright.

Murder Mansion

06 Murder Mansion
Difficulty level: Beginner – Intermediate

Core themes in horror films shift over decades based on what people consider frightening at the time. It's easy to spot trends from decade to decade and understand why older horror films scared audiences in the past but don't now.

Modern horror films that use too much violence are upsetting to watch because violence is a genuine threat in society today. In the '60s, people appear to have believed that covens of witches operated covertly among the 'normal' population, giving us classics such as *Rosemary's Baby*. In the '70s, a rise in reported possessions tingled the spines of God-fearing folk – thankfully we got beauties such as *The Exorcist* and *The Omen* out of it. Slasher films have been a constant over the history of horror, peaking with the likes of *The Texas Chainsaw Massacre* and one of the greatest horror pictures of all time – *Halloween*.

Eventually the horror genre became tired through overuse of clichés such as the virgin female victim, the masked silent murderer and the all-American high-school setting. Then along came *Scream*. Released in 1996 it breathed new life into the genre by knowingly playing up such clichés, while also managing to scare the wits out of us.

For me, the house from the final scene in *Scream* deserves a spot in the horrorgami canon. And just so that it doesn't appear too suburban, I've added some gruesome blood dripping from the windows and a shadowy figure in the doorway. Enjoy slashing your way through this one.

Cutting tips

The trickiest parts of this horrorgami are the dripping blood cut-outs. Don't attempt to cut them in one swoop as your knife will probably go off course. Cut them in tiny slices at a time. Start with those, then the windows; after that, the rest is fairly straightforward.

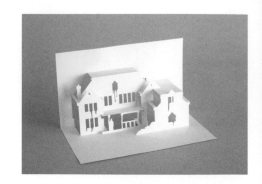

Folding

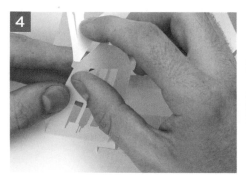

Start with the printed side facing you and push out the horizon valley folds.

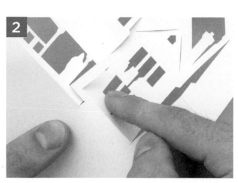

Push out the horizon folds at the base of the model.

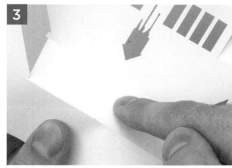

Rotate the model 180 degrees and push out the valley folds that join the rooftops to the background plane.

Flip the paper over and work your way through the mountain folds that join the gable ends of the house façades to the planes behind them. Start with the longer fold joining the main section of the house to the roof plane.

Turn the paper back over again to the printed side. Move on to the valley fold in the centre of the model (just under the bank of windows on the upper storey). Push the crease in with one hand while holding it with the forefinger and thumb of the other.

The previous fold will help everything come into shape. There are still a few folds to do in the middle part of the model. Work your way around them and then go over everything again before folding the model flat.

The Headless Horseman of Sleepy Hollow

07 The Headless Horseman of Sleepy Hollow

Difficulty level: Beginner – Intermediate

I loved Washington Irving's short story 'The Legend of Sleepy Hollow' as a kid. It recounts the story of the Headless Horseman, the ghost of a trooper decapitated in the American Revolutionary War who 'rides forth to the scene of battle in nightly quest of his head'.

But it was actually the Disney animated version that I found particularly enchanting. The main motivation for creating a horrorgami inspired by the tale of Ichabod Crane and the Headless Horseman (apart from creating a great visual) was the opportunity to include a kirigami-engineered bridge. Once you grasp the technique of producing a completely freestanding bridge from a single sheet of paper, the possibilities of the art form appear limitless

Cutting tips

Cut around the headless horseman character first and then move on to the fiery outline. Cut out the trees before tackling the structural lines.

Folding

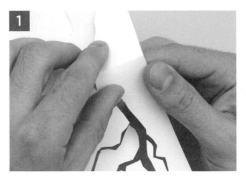

1

With the printed side facing you, start by lever-folding the main horizon valley folds on the left and right of the page.

2

Using the same technique, crease the two lever folds that attach the platform to the background plate. Take care that the paper doesn't snag against the decorative posts of the bridge.

3

Work your way across the front section of the model pushing out all of the valley folds that join the façades of the main platform to the base plate. Among these will be the two valley folds at the base of the bridge archway and two halfway up the front of the bridge.

4

Flip the paper over and, again, push out the mountain folds of the opposing valley folds you just creased. Only apply a small amount of pressure here. The model will start to take shape but the bridge will stop this from happening.

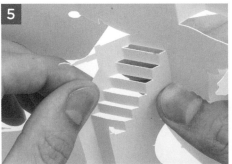

5

Use a springing action now to form the bridge steps. Hold the balustrade between your fingers in one hand and the front façade of the bridge in the other. Push the elements together and the steps will form. Repeat for the other side.

6

Finish the bridge by folding the crease at the base of the horse. At this point you should be ready to go over everything again before folding flat to complete the folds.

The Catacombs

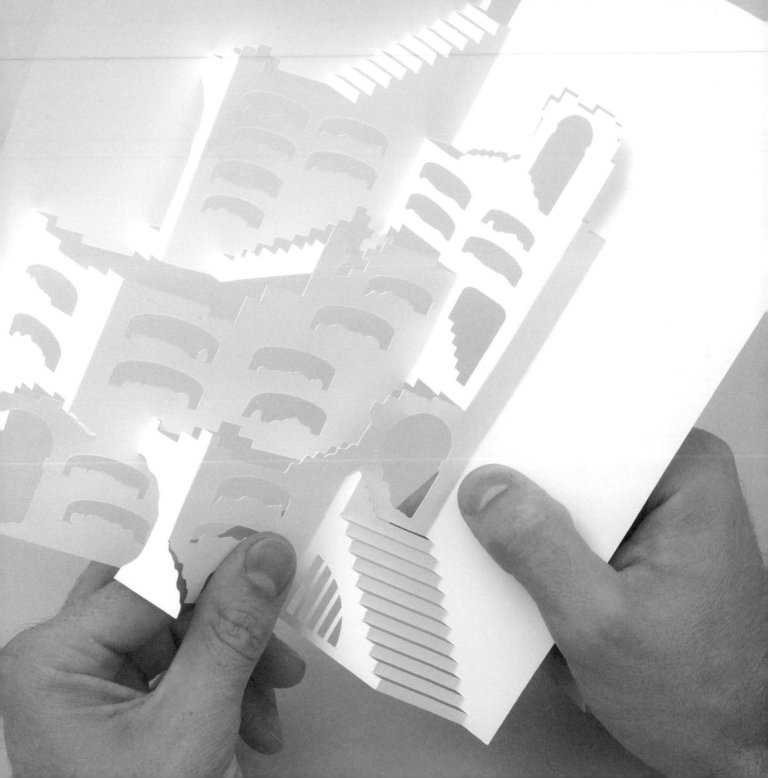

08 The Catacombs

Difficulty level: Intermediate

I can't think of a more nightmarish place to be trapped than in some dank, dark catacombs. This horrorgami is not strictly based on any one place but I've taken inspiration from a few different sources, mostly M. C. Escher. I'm a huge fan of Escher's impossible architectural constructions. His work pushes our concept of space and perspective, and encourages us to embrace concepts such as infinity.

Works such as *Relativity* and *Convex and Concave* have inspired this piece. Both of these lithographs depict cavernous spaces with stone arches and long staircases where points of origin and perspective seem to switch as your eye moves up them... or is that moves down them? Either way, it's impossible to pinpoint where this happens and the result is dizzying.

Escher's imagination can be seen as a major influence in many Hollywood films. In Christopher Nolan's *Inception* several of the sets can be directly linked to works by Escher, such as *Ascending and Descending*, in which a staircase winds round and round never seeming to get any higher. One of the final scenes in the classic fantasy film *Labyrinth* is based on Escher's *Relativity*.

Cutting tips

Although there's lots of cutting out in this model it's essentially straightforward. Start by cutting out all of the catacomb shelves before tackling the structural elements.

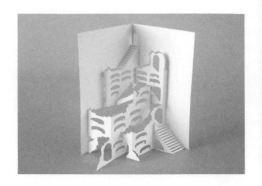

Folding

With the printed side facing up, start by pushing out the valley folds of the large lower staircase.

Directly above the top step is a long vertical valley fold that leads up to an arch near the top of the model. Again, push out this fold. Once there's enough give in it, you can pinch the two planes together to complete the fold.

Still with the printed side facing up, move across the paper and fold the far right valley fold. From here, work your way back over to the left, folding all of the valley folds on this side of the paper.

Now turn the paper over and crease the mountain fold on the far right that leads up to the top archway. It should be easy to fold the large lower staircase with a light springing action.

Again from the right, work across the paper, folding the various mountain folds. Leave the top staircase until the end.

Go over everything again before folding flat and opening to display.

A Haunted House

09 A Haunted House

Difficulty level: Intermediate

Ever wondered where the archetypal image of a haunted house came from? The houses in *Psycho*, *The Munsters*, *Beetlejuice*, *The Addams Family*, to name but a few, are all built in the style of Second Empire architecture, the period of rule under Napoleon III (1852–70). Tall mansard roofs stand almost vertical and are covered with rounded slate tiles interrupted by small dormer windows. The upper part, often almost invisible from the ground, is either flat or very slightly sloping. Wrought-iron cresting decorates the perimeter of the upper part of the roof. Elaborate bracketed cornices support a large cantilevered roof edge and tall windows with decorative moulding punctuate the horizontal lines of wood cladding. Arguably the most iconic feature – certainly in horror terms – is a tall, square tower either centrally placed or on the corner of the house. A raised platform covered by a shallow porch leads the way to a forbidding entranceway.

The style soon became a global trend, making its way to America during the late nineteenth century, and was adapted into less elaborate, but nonetheless lavish, domestic properties. After the Wall Street Crash and the Great Depression, many once-beautiful homes built during times of opulence were left abandoned. They became a symbol of depression and despair – actual ghost towns and thus the haunted house was born.

Cutting tips

This is a fairly easy horrorgami but the spaces in the railings will be a little laborious. You'll notice that there is a neat floating ghost in the porch. Take care you don't cut the small section that connects its head to the wall above. If you feel this is too advanced, it's fine to cut him off, the model will still look great – haunted or not.

Folding

With the printed side facing you, fold the main horizon valley folds and the two valley folds of the platform on which the house sits – they're located directly above them. Use the levering technique to do this.

Keep the printed side facing you and push out the valley folds at the base of the house. This includes the bottom of the veranda railings, the small railing section and the valley folds at the front door.

Turn the paper over and fold the mountain fold at the top edge of the veranda, including the small side section. This is the trickiest part. Use a very gentle pinching technique with one hand and pull the fold through from the opposite side of the paper with the other hand.

Begin creasing the mountain folds of the platform the house sits on. Hold the model in one hand and push the crease with the forefinger of the other hand. Flip the paper over again and use the same technique to fold the valley fold that forms the base of the same platform. Once you've done these, you can use a springing technique to fold the small set of steps.

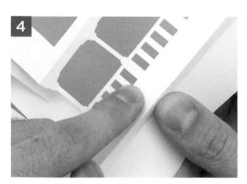

With the lower half of the model well on its way, concentrate on the mountain and valley folds of the roof section. There's no specific technique to use here, just a bit of prodding of fingers will do it.

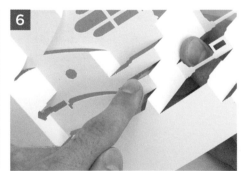

There are a couple of valley folds (A) that require specific attention. Once you've started all of the other folds this area will naturally head the way you want it. Just guide them into place as you fold it flat. Before you completely flatten the model to complete all the folds, go back to the top edge of the veranda and house platform and give them the once-over.

A

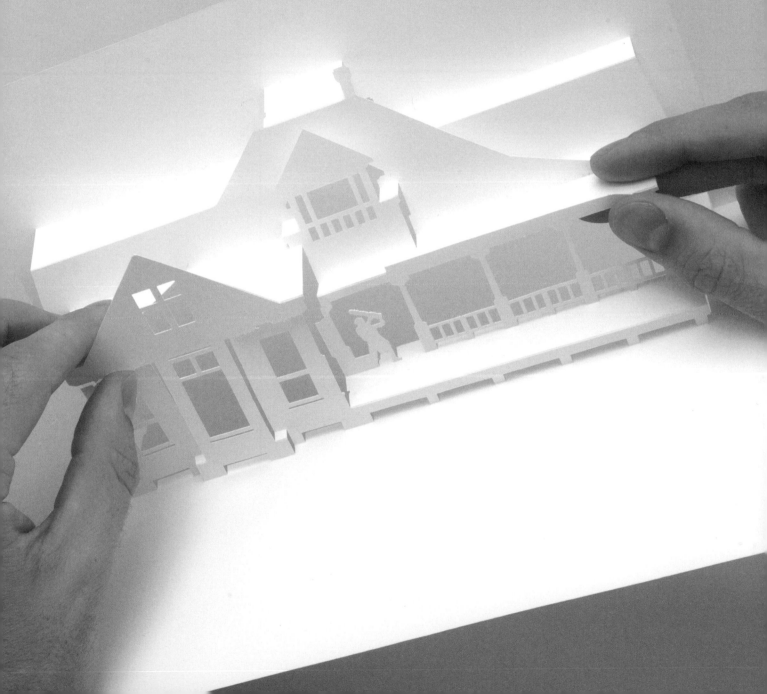

Farmhouse Bloodbath

10 Farmhouse Bloodbath

Difficulty level: Intermediate

This horrorgami is based on the house from *The Texas Chainsaw Massacre* – one of the most controversial horror films of all time. In fact, the uncut version was banned in the UK until 1999.

The film was shot on location in Round Rock, Texas. This humble, Queen Anne-style farmhouse provided the setting for Leatherface and his gruesome kindred. In 1998 the property was purchased by a hotel group, dismantled and relocated to Kingsland, Texas, where it now houses the Grand Central Café. So if you fancy spending the afternoon in the glorious surroundings of a former (fictional) slaughterhouse you could do no better than to visit. I'd pass on the 'meat' pie though.

Cutting tips

Start cutting around the character in the doorway first (A). It's OK to cut the blade of the saw in an irregular fashion. As you move along the line, push the tip of the blade into the paper while alternating the angle to give you a saw-toothed effect. The railings are on the slim side but if you take your time on them, the rest of the model cuts are plain sailing. Finally, as poetic as it may be, do not attempt to cut this horrorgami with a chainsaw. You'll ruin the dining table.

Folding

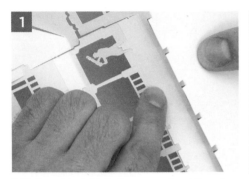

1 With the printed side facing you, push out the valley folds at the base of the building and the base of the porch. Hold the base plane in one hand and use a finger of the other hand to do this.

2 Rotate the model 180 degrees and fold the various sections of the roof that connect the model to the background plane. Lever-fold the one on the left, then the one on the right and then pinch the central fold.

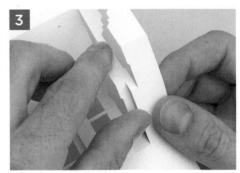

3 Rotate the model 180 degrees again and fold the horizon on the right-hand side, using the levering technique. Then, just below it, pinch together the two small valley folds.

4 Gradually work the rest of the folds until they become memory.

5 With the floor of the porch you can complete the mountain fold by holding the base plane flat in one hand and pressing the porch surface down onto the base with the other hand. Use a skewer to pull out the small sections near the base of the bay window.

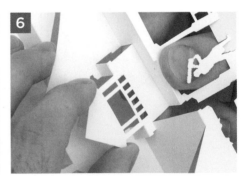

6 With the printed side facing you, push out the mountain fold that joins the porch roof to the base of the window, then the mountain and valley folds that join the window to the main roof façade. From the other side, put your right thumb under the doorway. Take the roof area between the chimneys between your left forefinger and thumb, and push the sections together in a springing motion until the paper gives.

A

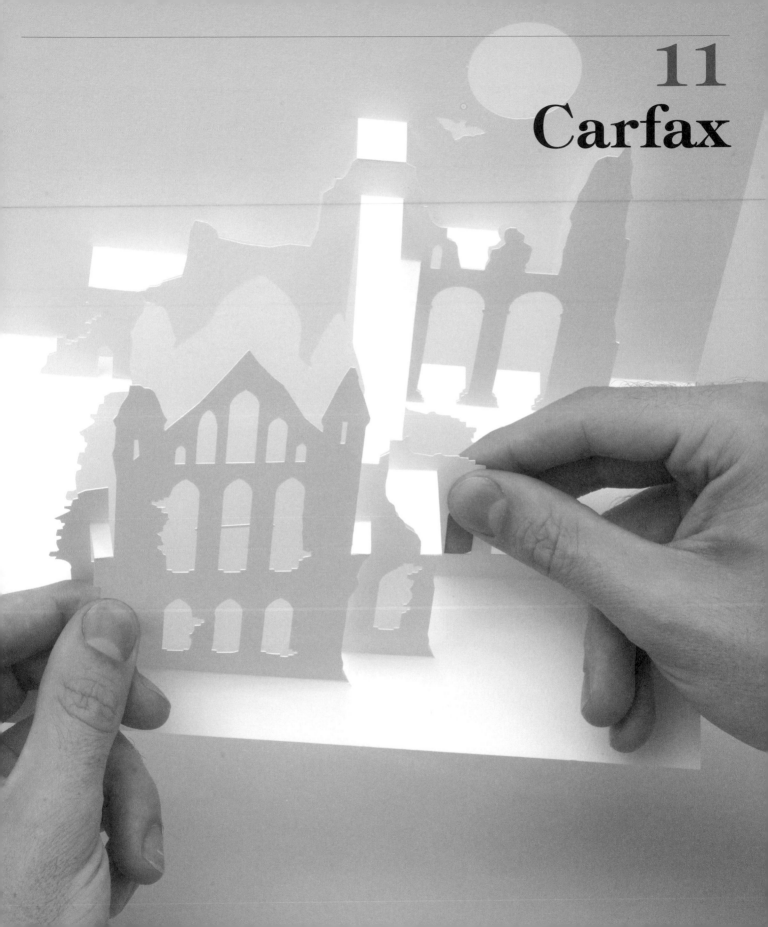

11 Carfax

Difficulty level: Intermediate

In Bram Stoker's novel *Dracula*, Carfax is the name of the estate in Purfleet just outside London that the Count buys and where he relocates. The purpose of solicitor Jonathan Harker's visit to Transylvania, mentioned in the novel, is to aid with the finalization of the transaction. The main residence at Carfax is described as being decayed, having been abandoned for some time, and having a church within its grounds.

Carfax doesn't exist, but it's commonly believed that Whitby Abbey on the coast of North Yorkshire, UK, provided Stoker with the inspiration for the Count's new abode. The abbey is the imposing ruin of a 700-year-old Benedictine monastery. When gazing upon its Gothic features and taking in its eerie atmosphere, it's easy to see how it could have inspired the original location in the novel.

Whitby Abbey also has a small church within its grounds. In other interpretations of the book, Carfax is renamed as Carfax Abbey, combining the church and main building into one.

Cutting tips

There are not so many straight-line cuts in this horrorgami but it's the jagged lines that will make it look like an authentic ruin. If they appear all too daunting, just use them as a guide. The more angular the cuts you use, the greater the impression of crumbling brickwork.

Folding

With the printed side facing you, start by creasing the main horizon valley folds, using the levering technique. Now work from left to right and push out the valley folds that make the background of the building (A).

Push out the valley folds on the base of the building in the foreground. Start with the main foreground section and then work backwards.

Rotate the paper 180 degrees and push out the three valley folds that join the background section of the building to the background plane.

Turn the paper over to the other side and fold the three opposing mountain folds of the three valley folds that you've just creased.

Moving back to the foreground section of the ruin, you can use a springing action to crease the mountain and valley folds that join the very front façade to the elements just behind it. This will now start to pull the whole structure forward.

Finally, turn to the long stretches of paper that connect the foreground cluster to the background. There's lots of room to get your fingers into this space, so use whatever technique feels comfortable. Go over everything again before folding flat.

12 The Werewolf

Difficulty level: Intermediate

The 1981 horror film *An American Werewolf in London* inspires this horrorgami. Originally I'd intended to create a model of the Slaughtered Lamb pub featured in the film but it just wasn't challenging enough. When I started to come up with ideas for this model I thought it would be interesting to switch the scene around and have a werewolf overlooking the small village where the pub was situated.

The film is most famous for its pioneering human-to-werewolf transformation. The make-up and prosthetics were developed by special-effects legend Rick Baker. I met Rick a couple of years ago in LA and was privileged to have been given a private tour of his incredible workshop (the interior of which is based on the Wicked Witch of the West's castle). It is full of puppets of the Gremlins, *Men in Black* aliens, *Grinch* costumes and of course the actual mask of the werewolf. Interestingly, due to budget constraints, the mask for the werewolf was created with an asymmetrical face so that the effect of two expressions could be shot from either side and the footage flipped.

Cutting tips

There are a lot of organic and jagged lines in this horrorgami. If it looks like they might drive you to lunacy, use them as a guide rather than being exact. It's much easier if you keep lifting the blade off the paper after each cut – especially around the fur of the werewolf. The jaggedness of the trees can mean the paper edges get caught against each other during folding, so be sure to keep your eye on them as you're folding and pop them out gently if they snag.

Folding

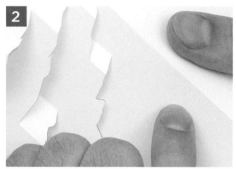

1 With the printed side facing you, start by folding the main horizon crease. Use the levering technique to do this. Push down the background plane with your forefinger and the base plane with your thumb while placing your middle finger in the valley of the fold for leverage.

2 Push out valley folds on the base of the mountains. The folds are quite tight around here so only apply a little pressure each time. Don't expect to complete the fold the first time. Take care around the town scene (A).

3 Rotate the horrorgami 180 degrees and use the springing technique to crease both the mountain and valley folds of the mountain edge on the left.

4 Lever-fold the valley fold that joins the cliff top to the background plane (B).

5 Work your way around the rest of the valley folds. The trickiest section is the area marked (C). You may want to use a skewer here to help pop out the mountain fold.

6 Flip the paper over and work on the mountain folds. Start with the two just to the right of the werewolf silhouette. You can lever-fold both of these. Finish with the mountain folds of the town – again, a skewer will really help here. You'll need to go back around everything again before folding everything flat.

Alien Abduction

13 Alien Abduction

Difficulty level: Intermediate

When I was a kid, my brother had a copy of *Mysteries of the Unexplained* published by Reader's Digest. That book provided a treasure trove of fantasies in which I would lose myself. Aside from articles about reported sightings of the Jersey Devil and Midwest exorcisms – standard interests of a 12-year-old – I was completely enchanted by the accounts of alien abductions and UFO sightings. On many occasions I convinced myself that I'd witnessed a genuine alien spacecraft, although when I was growing up in Northern Ireland in the '80s and '90s, the night sky was more likely to be filled with helicopters. That was irrelevant. I wanted to believe and I still live in hope.

Cutting tips

There are quite a few organic shapes in this model rather than straight lines so I'd start with the cow and the abductee while you're fresh. The cow's legs are quite thin, so be extra careful. After that, it's best to tackle the clouds, followed by the structural supports of the water tower. The actual folding part of the scene is quite simple and you'll probably find that the model will 'want' to fold itself in the right direction.

Folding

With the printed side facing you, fold the main horizon crease, using the levering technique. Push down the background plane with your forefinger and the base plane with your thumb, while placing your middle finger in the valley of the fold for leverage.

Push out the valley folds on the base; these include the barn, the shed and the bit where the spaceship tractor beam touches the ground.

Rotate the page 180 degrees and work your way across the various valley folds that connect the tops of the buildings to the background plane. Most of these are suited to levering, so place your index finger in the valley of the fold for leverage and push the two planes together with your forefinger and thumb.

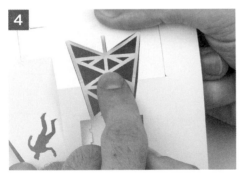

Be extra careful while folding the base of the water tank frame. Lever-fold the legs but use the finger of your other hand to push them out (A).

Turn the model over and work around the mountain folds. When folding the water tower, use a sliding technique to complete the crease. Keeping the background plane flat on the table with one hand, carefully grip the sides of the water tower with your forefinger and thumb of the other and pull away from the base plane. Repeat this action until there is enough give in the creases to fold flat.

Gently close the card flat. Press firmly down so that all the creases become memory. Open it up again and, only then, pop up the cow.

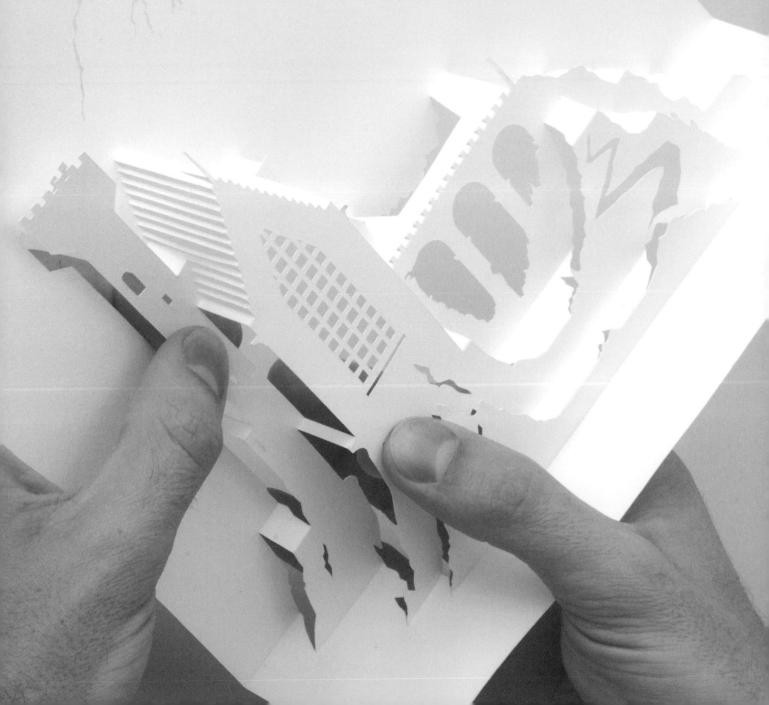

Dr Frankenstein's Watchtower

14 Dr Frankenstein's Watchtower

Difficulty level: Intermediate

From a dilapidated watchtower to a sprawling mansion, the style of the castle in Mary Shelley's *Frankenstein; or, The Modern Prometheus* from which Victor Frankenstein conducts his experiments has varied throughout the story's many incarnations since its publication in 1818. Although mostly refuted, links have been drawn between Burg Frankenstein in Darmstadt, Germany, and its inhabitant Johann Conrad Dippel, as the real inspiration for both the book's protagonist and his home. My horrorgami combines elements from many of the castle's incarnations – a lone, ominous and foreboding fortress clinging to a jagged mountain peak. Although the engineering of the paper is relatively simple, elements such as the lightning bolt and the winding path really bring this horrorgami to 'life'.

Cutting tips

If you want to freestyle your own lightning bolt, just try to finish the far left point in the same position that I have; then once folded it will line up exactly with the lightning conductor on the roof (A). The castellated turrets of the bridge (B) are quite laborious, so start there while you're fresh. Take extra care with the series of close parallel lines (C) that make up the pitched roof.

Folding

1 With the printed side facing you, start by lever-folding the main horizon.

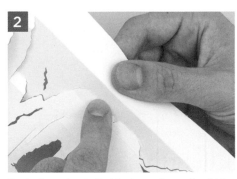

2 Gradually push out all of the base plane valley folds that make up the foot of the cliffs.

3 Work upwards through the valley folds on the back section of the model. A combination of pushing out folds and levering works best here.

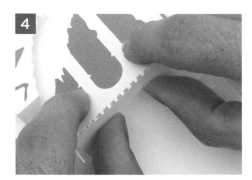

4 Turn the paper over and gently crease the mountain folds that make up the top of the cliff edges, including the bridge. As the section behind the bridge is cut away, you can use this to your advantage. Put your index finger behind the bridge (B) and apply a very soft pinching movement several times, teasing the fold until it becomes memory.

5 The long cuts in the pitched roof make the paper almost fabric-like and help them fold correctly. Hold the background plane flat with one hand and, with forefinger and thumb of the other, pull the front of the main building towards you until it is almost flat against the background plane. Repeat this gentle springing motion until the folds become memory and you can push the elements flat against each other.

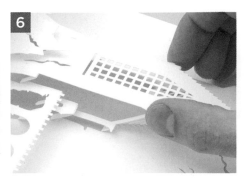

6 Go around all of the creases again before pressing the card flat and opening up the final model.

15
Dr Frankenstein's
Laboratory

15 Dr Frankenstein's Laboratory

Difficulty level: Intermediate

Dr Frankenstein's Laboratory is one of the most iconic sets in horror history. We're mostly familiar with depictions of a laboratory like that in the 1931 Universal Studios film and the multitude of sequels and parodies it spawned. It's easy to conjure a densely packed room of visual cues such as the monster lying on the operating table, bubbling chemical flasks, and huge Tesla coils. However, with this model, relying too much on cut-outs of electrical and chemical apparatus to make the scene would render it too difficult and too delicate to cut. So, in an effort to bring something new to the (operating) table I've focused more on the internal architecture of the room by adding Escher-inspired staircases and the large window featured in the Frankenstein Watchtower horrorgami on pages 87–91.

Much of what we think we know about Victor Frankenstein's laboratory was a Hollywood creation: for example, the Tesla coil was invented more than 70 years after Mary Shelley's novel was first published. The Hollywood assumption that electricity was involved may originate from the fact that in the book the lightning strike Victor witnesses inspires him to switch his studies from natural history to mathematics and science, thereby leading to his discovery.

Although Victor talks of how he 'dabbled among the unhallowed damps of the grave', the idea that he assembled his monster from a variety of stolen human body parts seems also to come from Hollywood. The novel describes how he 'collected bones from charnel-houses', suggesting that he first created a skeleton to his specification.

'As the minuteness of the parts formed a great hindrance to my speed, I resolved, contrary to my first intention, to make the being of a gigantic stature; that is to say, about eight feet in height, and proportionably large.'

Cutting tips

The detailing on this model is relatively modest. Take your time, though, on the area around the Tesla coils and the electric stream between the two. After that, the rest is a breeze.

Folding

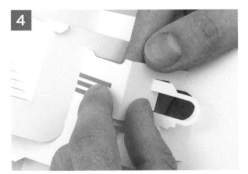

1

With the printed side facing you, use the levering technique to make the main horizontal folds. Then rotate the model 180 degrees and work your way around the valley folds that join the various platforms to the background plane.

2

Rotate the paper 180 degrees again and crease the valley folds that join the base staircase to its various floor levels (valley folds A, B and C); you can also fold the bases of the Tesla coils around the monster's operating table.

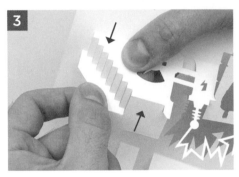

3

Turn the paper over, then use the springing technique to begin forming the staircase on the right. As you're doing this, start to pull up the pillar on the far right near the back of the model. As the crease becomes stronger it will help pull up the Tesla coils. Add a little more pressure there but don't complete the fold yet.

4

Swap between folding the mountain folds on the various platform tops on the left side and the valley fold at the base of the large central window.

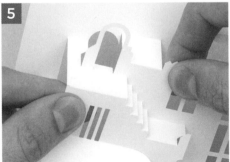

5

The trickiest bit is the upper staircase. Once the various folds have some give in them, you can complete the crease by holding the paper between your finger and thumb at the prison door and putting a finger down through the gap of the corrugated, sloping roof.

6

Work your way around the model, going over the folds again before folding flat. Finally, fold the two hinges on either side of the operating table. Before you display the model, put the tab at the end of the table through the slit to keep it in position.

Skull Island

16 Skull Island

Difficulty level: Advanced

Skull Island is the land that time forgot. Somehow this mythical place is still inhabited by creatures long thought to have been extinct. Once ruled by the awesome King Kong, the exact location of the island has again become legend, many speculating that it lies somewhere off the coast of west Sumatra.

King Kong is undoubtedly one of the most famous movie monsters ever created. Much like his peer, 'the monster' from *Frankenstein*, his character is portrayed as either a tragic and misunderstood antihero or a crazed and violent antagonist.

Cutting tips

Start with the skull features and then the pterodactyl flying in the background. Then go on to tackle the jagged mountain ranges.

Folding

With the printed side facing you, lever-fold the two horizon folds.

Directly above the two horizon folds are two more valley folds that attach the mountains in the background to the background plane – tackle these next. It's quite tight around here so it will help to place a skewer behind the fold and push against it with your forefinger and thumb. As you're doing this, the mountain folds directly in front of them will already start to form, but leave these for now.

Push out all of the valley folds that make up the base of the mountains on the base plane. Use a skewer behind the smaller rock formations in the foreground.

Turn the paper over. Move on to creasing the various folds around the skull area. There's room to put your finger in behind the skull and push it flat against the base plane.

Turn the paper over again. To the left and right of the base of the skull are two valley folds that join it to the background mountain range. Carefully pinch these together and, as you do this, everything else will start to come into shape.

Check over everything again a few times and fold flat.

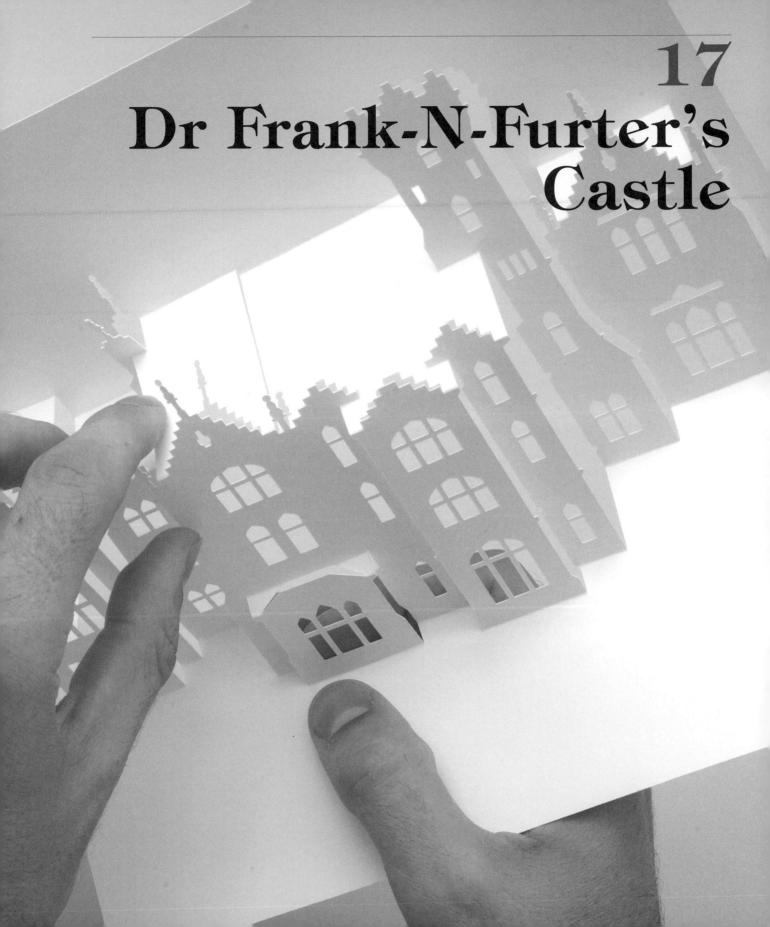

Dr Frank-N-Furter's Castle

17 Dr Frank-N-Furter's Castle

Difficulty level: Advanced

The Rocky Horror Picture Show (1975), which features the castle of mad scientist and transvestite Frank-N-Furter, was just one of many Hammer Horror-produced films that were shot on location at Oakley Court, a huge Victorian, Gothic-style manor situated in Berkshire, UK. The only difference between now and the time when *Rocky* was shot is the huge glass dome set upon the roof from which the rocket was launched at the end of the film.

At the time of production the building was in a dire state of repair but it has subsequently been restored as a luxury hotel. If you're tempted to turn up in your stockings and suspenders, check first that it's a 'Ladies' Night'.

Cutting tips

This horrorgami is mostly an intermediate level of difficulty; however, the spires on top of the roofs are particularly detailed and quite delicate, so take great care with them. While you're cutting and folding, be extra careful not to knock any of them off.

Folding

1 With the printed side facing you, use the levering technique to fold the main horizons.

2 Working from left to right, push out all of the valley folds that join the various front façades of the building to the base plane.

3 Rotate the paper 180 degrees and, as before, work from left to right, using the push-out folding technique for all of the valley folds that connect the rooftops to the background plane.

4 The tower (A) should naturally fold into shape, but a few quick lever folds will help it along.

5 Use the levering technique to crease all of the mountain folds that connect the roofs to the front façades.

6 Finally work on the two small bay windows (B) at the front of the castle. Use the sliding technique to push the plane upwards and flat against the plane behind. Work around the model again to complete the folds before closing the card and reopening to display the model.

Dracula's Castle

18 Dracula's Castle

Difficulty level: Advanced

This horrorgami is based on Bran Castle, located in southern Transylvania in central Romania. Count Dracula's castle is, of course, completely fictitious: there is no castle as mentioned in Bram Stoker's *Dracula* near the Borgo Pass in the Carpathian Mountains where the first part of the novel is set. The location Stoker picked was empty. Of course authors draw inspiration from different sources but many consider Bran Castle in particular to have played a major role in the imagining of the Count's terrifying stronghold.

Although Stoker never actually visited Romania, he was said to be aware of the castle after having seen an illustration in a book by Charles Boner. The description of the fortress in the novel is strikingly similar to the real Bran Castle; no other castles in Romania match the description.

During the time Stoker spent researching European folklore and Romanian history, he became aware of the warlord Vlad III, Dracula of Wallachia on whom it is said Count Dracula was based. The name Dracula translates as 'Son of the Dragon' or 'Son of the Devil'. This, coupled with Vlad's infamous reputation for murder and torture, seemed to be a good enough reason for Stoker to change the principal character's name from Count Wampyr to Count Dracula. Several references in the book to the Count's own past are similar to the recorded history of Vlad III. Due to the character's history being blended with folklore, legend, and factual references to Vlad III, Count Dracula has managed to live on beyond the novel and earn his place in horror history.

Legend aside, Bran Castle is a truly remarkable building: fused into the jagged mound, it looks as if it has grown from the rock and is the closest thing you'll get to a fairy-tale castle – albeit a rather gruesome one.

Cutting tips

Start with the staircase that leads up into the castle. Push the blade down into the paper and then repeat, switching the angle each time to create the steps.

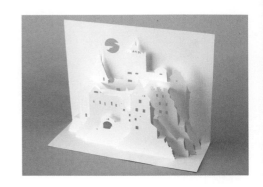

Folding

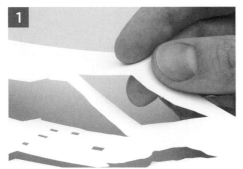

1

With the printed side facing you, start by lever-folding the main horizon valley folds on the left and right of the page.

2

Work your way from left to right, creasing all of the valley folds at the base of the mountain. There are seven in total.

3

Rotate the page 180 degrees and push out the four valley folds that attach the castle to the background plane. Work your way from top to bottom pushing out all of the valley folds. You can use a springing technique to fold the small connection between the two towers in the foreground.

4

Flip the paper over and begin working on the mountain folds. All of the folds on the right-hand side of the model can be creased using the springing technique to push the different planes of paper together again, particularly the staircase that runs right up to the turret section of the castle.

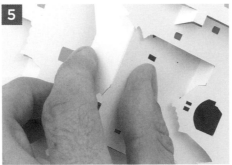

5

With your finger behind the fold, pinch together the mountain fold (A) in the centre of the model.

6

Go over everything again before folding the card flat to complete the folds.

The Ghost Train

19 The Ghost Train

Difficulty level: Advanced

I adore ghost trains. I'll even sit in a heightened state of glee throughout the really naff ones you find in travelling fairgrounds. You know, the sort with dodgy animatronics and a finale that usually involves someone jumping out wearing a zombie mask bought from the thrift store.

A ghost train is a type of 'dark ride', a fairground ride in which punters journey through an enclosed, artificially lit environment. Slow-moving carriages take them past a variety of illuminated scenes enhanced with music, other sounds, and special effects. Dark rides began appearing in the late 1800s and were originally magical or romantic experiences. It wasn't until 1930 that the concept of a dark ride acquired a more sinister and spine-chilling connotation.

My very first experience of a ghost train was that at the Blackpool Pleasure Beach, UK, which was also the home of the first ghost train. My Ghost Train horrorgami is a celebration of all things creepy and locomotive.

Cutting tips

By this stage you should be pretty confident with your cutting. The railings are very narrow on this horrorgami but the most laborious task is the cresting on the roof. Start there, followed by the skull, and then work your way outwards. You can always leave the railings in and just cut the basic outer shape, if you're not 'brave enough'.

Folding

With the printed side facing you, push out the valley fold that joins the roof plane to the background. The valley folds to the immediate left and right (A) can then be lever-folded.

Flip the paper over. The small but many mountain folds along the cresting of the roof will begin to take shape after the first fold. Squeeze the roof façade and background together between your fingers and thumb.

Flip the paper back over. Begin with levering the main horizon valley folds and move down the paper folding the other two pairs of valley folds that join the building to the base until you reach the steps in front of the façade.

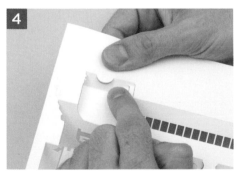

Push out the front of the steps (B) on both sides. Then work upwards, pushing, pinching and levering the rest of the valley folds. Use your intuition to figure out when to begin alternating between the valley and mountain folds to help the model take shape.

Fit your forefingers through the space left behind by the railings and pinch them towards the base.

Use a skewer to pop out the train carriages and leave it in place while clawing the section together. The skewer will stop the paper from folding in on itself in the wrong direction. Work around the model again to complete the folds before closing the card and reopening to display the model.

Monster Attack

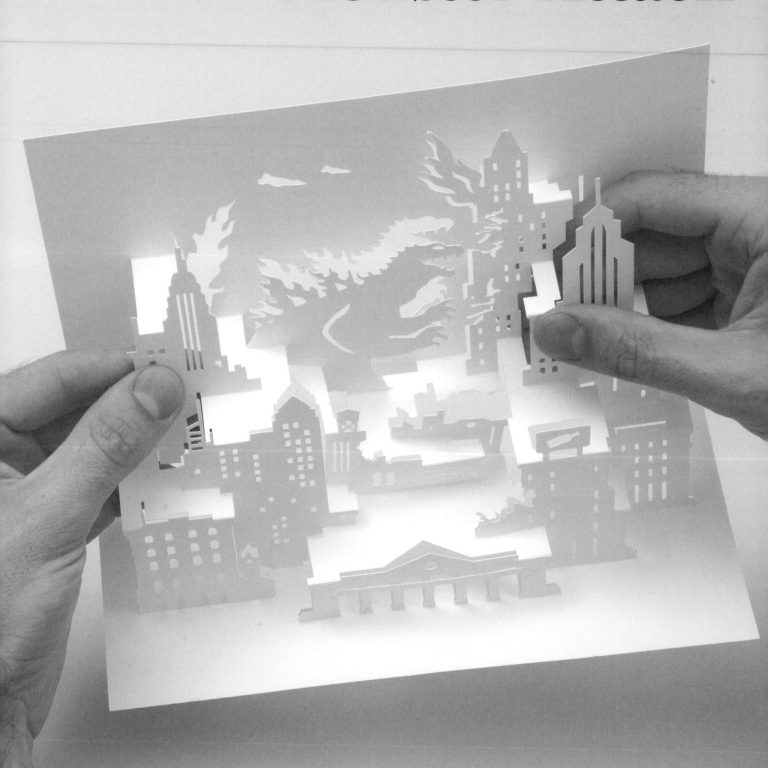

20 Monster Attack

Difficulty level: Advanced

I love a good monster movie. This piece is an homage to the old black-and-white Godzilla films, and modern ones like *Cloverfield*, which I must say made me really motion sick in the cinema. Godzilla first appeared on screen in a 1954 Japanese film and is more a cultural icon now than a mere movie monster. It is one of the few monsters that is portrayed as either a destructive antagonist or misunderstood protagonist, but Godzilla is the only monster with a star on Hollywood Boulevard.

I won't pretend that I stay calm when I make a mistake halfway through a model. In fact, I've been known to throw huge tantrums, so it feels right that this final horrorgami will have the potential to release your inner monster – especially if the knife slips right at the end.

Cutting tips

When I was designing this horrorgami I wanted to avoid straightforward lines on building edges, so you will need to keep changing the direction of your knife – there are lots of small cut-outs and funny shapes. If you want to leave out a bunch of windows, that's fine; if you want to add in more, that's even better! Feel free to simplify the funny-shaped lines. Start with the monster (A), followed by the flames (B) and the damaged part of the buildings. After that, begin working on as many of the windows as you want.

Folding

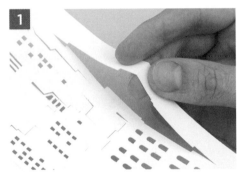

With the printed side facing you, lever-fold the main horizon crease.

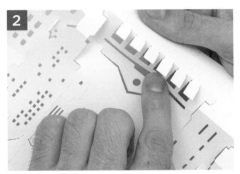

Push out the valley folds that join the facade of the buildings to the base plane including the area with the portico.

Move on to the top valley folds where the roofs of the buildings join the background plane.

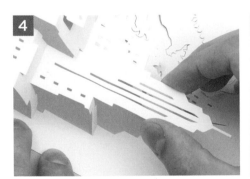

Flip the paper over and fold the rooftop mountain folds. Use the springing technique for the flaming building in the background and the building just to its right.

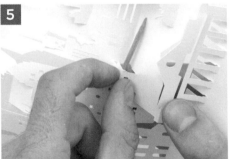

The trickiest section is in the centre of the model and to the right of the small water tower. Apply just a small amount of pressure to the folds, using a skewer, and repeat until there is sufficient give. Place your thumb behind the peaked roof of the portico. Use two fingers of the same hand to support the walls of the building that sits on its roof; with the other hand, pinch together the creases of that area.

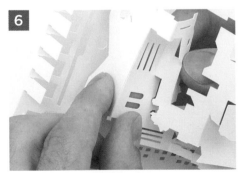

Flip the paper over and fold the rest of the valley and mountain folds before carefully folding the model flat.